On Wealth

Alan Boone

ISBN: 1490980466
ISBN-13: 978-1490980461

DEDICATION

To my family

Contents

ACKNOWLEDGMENTS

Initially, it may seem that an essay is a nothing but free flowing opinion. Yet opinion comes from a long line of people and facts that have gone into creating it. Hopefully the opinions contained herein are logical. I must acknowledge the teachers that I had in school from grades one through twelve, who opened up whole worlds of inquiry; the liberal arts college that I attended, which encouraged broad inquiry into multiple fields of learning and critical thinking; the professors who devoted time and individual attention to the needs of the student; and my mother, who read to me as a child.

PREFACE

What is wealth, and does it really measure a person's worth? What does it measure? This is the question that led to this essay. It is worth noting that this is an essay and not a treatise. As such, it relies more on common knowledge, than research. Everything written in this essay is therefor subject to research and further inquiry, and I strongly encourage that.

Personal wealth is a measure of what a person takes out of society and uses for himself. Contribution to society may be measured by other means, but it cannot be measured by accumulated personal wealth. Once the question has been asked, it is necessary to place it in the context of history, society, culture, morality, religion, and sundry economic systems. How should and how does personal wealth relate to societal wealth? Finally, how does emerging technology affect the distribution of wealth? Today, as never before, technology holds the promise of eliminating the need for work in all fields of endeavor. By eliminating the drudgery of work, it also eliminates the means by which wealth has been distributed for millennia. What is the future of wealth and society? We can examine it, but we cannot predict it.

One thing is certain. No one's self worth can be measured in monetary terms. Likewise, neither can anyone else's.

PART ONE
Defining Wealth

Personal Wealth

Defining personal wealth is difficult. Three things make it difficult. First, it is relative. Second, it is a matter of perception. Third, it is always changing. An individual in a refugee camp may view someone with a coffee pot as wealthy. An individual with a nice bungalow may view someone with a mansion as wealthy. An individual with a mansion may consider someone with several mansions around the world and a yacht to be wealthy. As economies and personal situations change, so does the perception of wealth.

1) Clearly the perception of wealth is relative, and wealth itself may be relative to the society. The accumulation of livestock and wives was often the measure of the wealth of kings, and may still have sway in some societies today. A society with a

middle class and a relatively even distribution of its wealth is a fairly new idea in the world. This idea has been largely promoted in the United States since its founding based on the idea that all men are created equal. However, it is not unique in the world.

For millennia, it was understood that wealth was the purview or even the God given right of kings, landowners, and others of power. Masses of slaves and other workers labored to generate the wealth that rightfully belonged to the nobles. This right to wealth was passed down by inheritance, usually to the first born son. The right of primogeniture, which gave everything in the estate to the firstborn son, continued in English law through the centuries. This tended to preserve the estate. De Tocqueville felt that getting rid of the right of primogeniture, and subdividing estates in the U. S. forced generations to seek wealth outside of their inheritance and furthered democracy in the U.S.

2) Because wealth is such a fluid concept, it is necessary to reach a definition of wealth in order begin any study of it. The properties of a bucket of water cannot be analyzed if you are trying to hold the water in your fingers. It is necessary first to create the bucket. Here is where honest men can differ greatly, but let's start with a few assumptions. First, let's narrow the definition to present day America. All of the principals established apply equally to all societies and times, but for this discussion let's consider only the here and now.

So how would we describe a wealthy individual? Is it in terms of assets or of income? The best definition that I have heard of a wealthy individual is someone who does not have to go into work every day because of his assets. In addition, one must have the ability to live opulently when compared to, well…. you. People who are retired are not considered wealthy living off of social security and retirement savings. One must have sufficient assets of his own to live off of them without additional revenue. In other words, assets, excluding retirement, turn out to be the measure of personal wealth. Assets, in turn generate income, and allow for an opulent lifestyle.

The exact breaking point between poverty, middle class wealth, and exceptional wealth will remain undefined.

3) Change happens. The average person of today is far wealthier than the average person of the past, or even the wealthier person of the past. Commonly, people are not on the edge of poverty and even starvation as has been so prevalent in past centuries. Technology and the constant progress of mankind has drastically changed our definition of wealthy. Since wealth is a variable that depends on societal context and perception, and because it is constantly changing, a precise definition is not necessary.

Societal Wealth

Let us turn for a moment from personal wealth to societal wealth, or the aggregate wealth of individuals as a group.

Wealth and power are synonymous. Although they are often discussed as if they were two different things, they correlate together well. The power to walk into a yacht showroom and to walk out with a yacht is great power, and it derives from money. Money buys political influence and access to power. This has been true throughout history.

Let's begin with a hunter gatherer society. It would not take long for any group of people to realize that more can be accomplished as a group than individually. In fact it is not hard to imagine that man quickly realized that survival itself depended on group cooperation. However, where groups form, someone must lead. There are probably as many ways to create the leadership of the group as there are groups. Physical strength, warrior status, or accomplishments are ways to select a leader. Early in man's history, groups recognized the value of experience, and frequently tribes were led by the elders.

Personal wealth often accompanied the leadership role, but societal wealth depended not on the ability of an individual to succeed within the group, but the ability of the group to accomplish goals together. As populations grew, organization became increasingly difficult, and business, commerce and government became more complex and sophisticated in response.

In a hunter-gatherer society, the ability to hunt or gather more effectively would logically lead to personal wealth within the society. If the tribe were better at it on the whole, it would lead to societal wealth. As with all wealth, it would be subject to the vicissitudes of circumstance. Droughts, storms, and migrations could lead to loss of societal wealth. The ability to follow herds or resources as they moved became a necessity. As tribes encountered scarcity, the ability to wage war also became important, requiring new skills, social values, and organization. Bravery and prowess in hunting could easily translate to warrior skills.

As with all wealth, environmental destruction quickly followed. The Pyrenean ibex was hunted to extinction by early man. The finite earth always seemed able to accommodate the quest for wealth with new discoveries of land and resources. Not surprisingly, man always believed that this could continue forever.

Then came agriculture. Since agriculture and written language appeared on the scene almost simultaneously, it is difficult to determine which came first. These two pillars of civilization changed the nature of wealth. Private property, especially land became important. This remained the purview of kings for millennia. Human interaction did not change, but the measures of success and the means of achieving it did.

Shortly, in historic terms, men of power organized to increase their power and wealth. This was done by conquest of land and of other men. Better organization, discipline, and sheer overwhelming manpower allowed men to conquer and rule ever larger areas and populations. This led to the early great empires. Success snowballed, as the national wealth of empire in the form of slaves, precious metals, and other resources accumulated.

Babylonia, Assyria, Egypt, even Greece and Rome grew on the backs of the great resource, slaves. It took the industrial revolution to change the inherent wealth generating potential of slavery and to change basic human culture on the subject. As with all things, the desire for wealth seemed to be the driving force, and as with all things, the old ways die hard.

Although slavery was a human institution for thousands of years, in the late 18th century mankind began to question its morality. The question arose during the founding of the United States, but was set aside for until the country had existed long enough to survive. The issue of slavery was not settled in the United States until the mid-nineteenth century.

Many believe that slavery was an American institution, but it was simply something that was brought to America from the lands that delivered settlers to our shores. The institution was so pervasive that many Native American tribes took captives for slaves. In fact, the United States is the only nation that paid a great price in blood to eliminate slavery within its boundaries.

Yet slavery in some forms still exists in the world today, and, as in the past, in the interest of profit.

How is societal wealth distributed once it is generated? Since the beginning of man, wealth has been distributed by simply taking it. This grew the wealth of early kings and emperors, but was probably different only in scale from the way wealth was distributed in a state of nature.

Not contributing in some way to the wealth of the tribe, if only by not killing or gathering your own food, would also generate no personal wealth. However, from the beginning, the ability to take wealth through commerce or by force, allowed the ability to have wealth without equal contribution to the society.

In theory, wealth goes to those willing to work for it. Taking it by conquering slaves and resource rich lands is not going to be accomplished without great effort and organizational skills. According to the classical theories of economics from Adam Smith forward, work entitles one to the fruits of their labor Apples on the tree or on the ground belong to no one until someone exerts the labor to pick them. Crops must be planted, nurtured and harvested. Sheep and cattle must be tended. Metals must be mined. The collective effort of society has always been the source of the collective wealth of the society. Even human capital in the form of slaves needed to be harvested by the Roman legions.

Still, once generated, wealth remained in the hands of the few able to take it. From tribal chieftains to early kings wealth came to them through conquest, taxes or tribute. In return for loyalty, military service, and tribute, the kings offered protection.

In the 16th through 18th centuries, a system of societal wealth existed in the form of mercantilism. The basic premise was that a nation gained societal wealth by making sure that more goods came into the country than left it. With the value of gold, silver, and spices enhanced by scarcity, this included accumulation of those items. Today, we might call this a favorable balance of trade. This encouraged colonialism, and European nations struggled to establish and hold colonies. Wars resulted.

Actually, there seems little difference between the mercantilism and colonialism of 17th century Europe and the rapacious colonialism of Rome or Assyria. In the end all such powers run up against the limit of their growth when they reach a power of equal or greater capabilities. The history of man is written in blood as nations and empires marched back and forth across the same lands, challenging each other as they went. As with Spain, England and France, nations throughout history have also faced economic ruin from overreaching in war. This is a lesson, the United States can ignore only at its peril.

Throughout history, the question of how to distribute societal wealth within the community has remained a social issue. Traditionally, it has always gone to the powerful and already wealthy until some form of revolt tears the society apart. From the slave revolt of Spartacus to the French revolution to the revolt against the Tsar in Russia, the theme plays out repeatedly and frequently.

History shows a shift of wealth from kings and generals, to slave owners, to large landowners, to factory owners, to those who owned railroads or oil, to software owners. Rapidly changing technology has in recent years allowed for the quick accumulation of wealth to a previously unimaginable degree. Indeed, today it is essential to accumulate wealth rapidly, for the slightest hesitation results in the marketplace moving on to the next big thing. You must grab the wealth of your society quickly or they will give it to someone else.

Another large segment of society is able to siphon off wealth without contributing any product. It is easy to argue the value of a public banking system and private bankers. It is harder to show that they contribute according to the level of wealth that they receive in return for their services. Likewise insurance companies contribute to society, but is their contribution equal to their profits? Every company needs a CEO, but are the salaries paid to

American CEOs in proportion to their contribution? The argument that they need to pay huge salaries to get good CEOs is specious at best. At worst, it is self-serving unmitigated nonsense.

Does a relationship between personal and societal wealth exist? If a relationship between personal contribution to society and personal wealth existed, you could argue that wealth is being equitably distributed. If the member contributed greatly to the tribe and was greatly rewarded for it, the distribution would be fair. However, there appears to be an inverse relationship between individual wealth and societal wealth. This is not new. The wealth generated by slaves was at one time the great contribution to societal wealth. They didn't get to keep it. Instead it went to great kings and landowners. Not much has changed.

If we are to determine if personal wealth and societal wealth have a relationship, we must first measure both. Obviously, this is not easy to do. Even before we get to that question, we need to understand what we are measuring in both cases. What is a contribution to society? What is personal compensation for that contribution?

First let's be clear about what wealth measures. Although our society uses it as a measure of status and value, what personal wealth really measures is the amount that an individual takes out of his society and keeps for himself. It does not measure an individual's contribution to society, which must be measured by a different and more difficult metric.

Employers often say and sometimes want to believe that pay is related to contribution to the company. It is not necessarily the case. It is not the case on a macro-economic (international and national) basis, and it is not the case on a micro-economic (individual business) basis. There is a disconnect between contribution and reward.

Payment for labor is partially a function of supply and demand, but as everyone who has been in the work force knows, it is related more to self-promotion than to productivity. Many efforts have been made to objectivize pay systems. They all seem to be based on the idea that an aggregate set of numbers developed by a lot of small subjective judgments is superior to a single subjective judgment about the employee. The greater the number of subjective judgments that go into the process, the better the results are considered to be. The reality is that a great deal of management time is used for the process and the results are no less subjective than in the past.

On the level of the society as a whole, there is also no relation between contribution and a level of compensation that leads to wealth. Perception matters. Who contributes more to society? Is it the highly compensated owners, CEOs, rock stars, sports stars, movie stars, beneficiaries of large estates, or lucky gamblers? Is it the less compensated teachers, police officers, fire fighters, caregivers, nurses, and social workers? Is it the farmer, the laborer, the technician, the homemaker, the mechanic? What is their contribution? The salesman is often compensated more than the ones who produce and service the product being sold.

How do you measure relief of suffering, the satisfaction of a McDonald's customer, a smile on a child's face, public safety, individual security, a full stomach, entertainment, or imparted knowledge and wisdom? What about the inventor or the innovator? History shows that the inventor is not as likely to benefit from his invention as the one who can skillfully manipulate patents and franchises. Benefits accrue to the one most able to commercially market what is often someone else's idea.

This is not to say that the wealthy do not contribute as much as they receive in wealth. First, contribution is hard to measure, and second, there is not a relationship between contribution and compensation. Yet you could argue that the incremental happiness that Michael Jordan contributed to his loyal fans add up to more than he has received in the compensation that led to his personal wealth. The economic contributions of Henry Ford, John D. Rockefeller, and Henry Kaiser may well have exceeded their personal wealth. Henry Kaiser was especially interesting because of his contributions to both business, government, and society during WW II.

Because of the difficulties of measuring contribution, it is easier focus only on the measurable accumulation of wealth.

Accumulation is a key to growth in assets and wealth, since one would be wealthy regardless of compensation if they gave away every penny they took in. Therefore, we have to return to the definition of wealth. It is not what one takes in, but what one keeps for himself. Further, frequently wealth is gained by non-productive or even counterproductive means. Some paths to wealth include immoral and occasionally illegal means. Drug dealing, pornography, fraud, theft, Ponzi schemes, and insider trading are some illegal paths to wealth. Other paths to wealth may be questionable but not illegal. Tobacco and alcohol have generated great wealth in the past. Even though tobacco is merely a delivery system for the addictive drug nicotine, Duke University gets its name from old tobacco money, and alcohol has generated many a fortune.

Other ways to wealth are neither immoral nor illegal but have little productive value. These paths include inheritance, the lottery, owning a piece of property that suddenly without contribution from the owner grows in value. Going to Antiques Roadshow and finding you have a million dollar item makes you a sudden millionaire. You have contributed nothing to society.

Wheeling and dealing, or buying low and selling high contribute nothing to society, yet can gain one a great deal in assets. If it is pure luck and a surprise, it is not immoral, but in how many cases wealth is generated by cheating either the one from whom something is purchased or the one it is sold to.

Speculative investments are another road to wealth. You may speculate on commodities, real estate, oil, gold, factories, or the results of a horse race. During the last fuel price "crises", I spoke with someone at the gas station where I was filling my tank. He said he was filling up because it was predicted that prices were going to go to $5.00 per gallon. He was blaming the problem on "those speculators" that were hoarding oil and gasoline in anticipation of the price rise. Meanwhile, he was filling his tank and all of his gas cans completely oblivious to the fact that speculating was exactly what he was doing. With everyone reacting the same way, it is no wonder the price of gasoline was spiking at the time.

Much wealth can be generated by creating a false bubble, sometimes by well-placed rumors. This works only if you can sell before the bubble bursts. The crash of 2008 was driven by a bubble in the real estate industry. This bubble was created and exaggerated by the banking industry. The repeal of the Glass-Stigall Act in 1999 took away the constraints which kept investment banking separate from commercial banking. This allowed banks to speculate wildly with the small depositor's money. Wall Street added to the speculation on the high risk real estate that was creating the bubble. While selling this to investors, they themselves bet on the failure of the same investments. This created a bubble that burst in 2008. Wall Street bankers still got their bonuses, even though they not only failed to contribute to the society, but also created a major negative impact on their nation.

This points to another aspect of great wealth. In many (perhaps most such cases) great wealth results from a willingness to take from those around you without making a contribution to them. Investment bankers are just one group. The larger the organization, the easier it is to receive without giving. Enron is not the only big business in its class. It just got caught in a more public failure. Bankruptcy not only protects investors and creditors, it also protects perpetrators of large fraud.

Enron was an energy company whose management Many articles were written about how much those who worked at Enron were making, from the secretary to the management. Their retirement plans were said to be second to none and every single Enron employee was expected to retire wealthy. Later anecdotal reports and some recordings surfaced about Enron employees laughing about defrauding "little old ladies" of their life savings. Meanwhile financial reports were being falsified, and energy prices were being manipulated. In the end, investors and the public had been defrauded of an estimated $74 billion. Unfortunately investor and consumer fraud is not an unusual story.

Wall Street has also had its share of scandal. Bernie Madoff was the owner of another well known investor that was perceived to be very successful. When his schemes unraveled, many lost their life savings and he eventually went to prison.

After nearly bringing the world's economy to its knees in 2008, investment bank CEOs and other leaders had the audacity to argue that they needed excessive compensation to attract "good" people and to avoid a brain drain to other countries. Considering the incredible amount of damage that they had done to their fellow Americans, it seems that such a brain drain would have done a great service to the nation.

Having dealt with the disconnect between contribution and reward, let's consider for a moment the impact wealth may have upon the individual. A wise college dean once told me that one of the benefits of being an educator is that you never have enough money to spoil your kids. Some parents have had to grieve over the loss of a child in an expensive muscle car that they gave him. Kennedys have been lost as a result of doing things that the average person could never afford to do. Lives have been lost on Everest because some people were rich enough to buy the opportunity to see the top of Everest. Why are so many wealthy celebrities lost to drugs and alcohol?

Let us stipulate that many individuals are able to handle wealth well. Unfortunately many don't. Wealth allows one to participate in dangerous activities for fun. Activities such as mountain climbing, racing, and possibly skiing require wealth in order to participate. Drugs and alcohol are also dangerous activities that can be indulged by those who are wealthy enough to participate. Although you can easily argue that these are also activities of the poor, the wealthy can indulge without having to cut back on food and rent or break into houses. Nonetheless, there are consequences.

But let us say that the wealthy engage in none of the activities that pose a danger to themselves and those around them. Are there other consequences? It has been my experience that the wealthy, even those who were once poor, are unable to relate to the difficulties of those around them who struggle daily to make ends meet. It is the opinion of most of the well-off people I know, that the poor are poor only because of their laziness and bad choices. There is no room in their hearts for those who are victims of circumstances.

Wealth can have a debilitating effect on those who are so blessed. It can cripple their souls when it comes to compassion and understanding. If you discuss compassion with many wealthy individuals, it is easy to see why Christ said that it is hard for a rich man to enter the Kingdom of Heaven. It is possible, but only if they can achieve a perspective about their wealth.

PART TWO
The Role of Business

Business and commerce have been part of human society as long as there has been human society. Commerce has existed since the first time someone decided to peacefully obtain something desired from another who possessed it. I'll give you part of the deer I just killed, if you will give me those pretty shells you found. Quickly, mankind developed agriculture and manufacturing. Otzi, the five thousand year old European found preserved in the glaciers of Europe, was using arrows that were created by a manufacturing process. Some were in varying stages of completion.

Business and commerce perform crucial social needs. It provides the organization necessary to perform functions. The hunter provides food to the tribe, and his contribution of the deer meat creates reimbursement in the form of shells which provide a need for some beauty and variety in his surroundings. The gatherer of the shells provides the other need, in return for which he receives some food in the form of the venison.

Rational men quickly realized that more can be accomplished by organizing into groups than by individuals alone. An individual might not be able to bring down a mammoth, but an organized group of hunters might. Thus organized business grew. As with most development and innovation, this had the capacity for both good and ill. Human nature being what it is, the organization into businesses could produce both good results and greed.

Early business produced the basic needs of food, shelter, and clothing. Once those needs were met, man quickly began to develop science, arts, entertainment and creature comforts. The uneven distribution of wealth to the powerful kings allowed such personal indulgences as elaborate tombs, pyramids, and cool hanging gardens. The introduction of mediums of exchange took commerce to a new level, allowing for banking and money lending. Commercial transactions could be handled unscrupulously without the action of an outside force such as morality, religion, or enlightened self-interest. When all else failed, government has long been used to enforce the morality that the populace was either unwilling or unable to live up to.

As businesses and governments grew in size and complexity, the impact on societal economies grew in relation. Today big business and big government have unprecedented power to control economic events. Hopefully each will exercise enough countervailing power to balance the other. Absolute control of despotic powers over your life and economic affairs is the basic battle line between American conservatives and liberals today. Conservatives fear absolute power by government but seem willing to yield absolute power to billionaire businessmen, while liberals seem to fear business but not government.

The history of man so far has indicated that business and the related technological development has served man well and increased the quality of life at all levels. The result has been an unprecedented ability to meet the requisite social needs, especially in America. We would do well to carefully examine those things that business does well and replicate them, while reining in on those things in which they do a disservice to society.

We know that business can benefit society. It can do this by efficiently providing that which is needed or desired by the society. Society itself is a conglomerate of customers. Once the needs of those customers have been satisfied, they begin to seek their wants. When the wants have been satisfied, to the extent that they have been satisfied in most industrialized nations, new wants have to be created through marketing. It is not hard to induce a want in a society when its needs and natural wants have already been met.

Thus business meets the needs of society by providing the needs of the customer. Businesses used to have to compete for customers. Now they compete in congress for special legislation to limit their competition, or provide subsidies, or protect them from their mistakes. Banking, insurance, and auto manufacturer bailouts are examples of the latter. They know that if you can grow large enough, congress will consider you too big to fail. This is a goal that is far from customer service.

It is also obvious that there are some business activities that do not serve society by serving the customer. Some are strictly prohibited by government. Murder for hire has been judged by society to be a prohibited business endeavor even though it provides a profit while serving a customer. Society expects government to enforce the ban. Drug dealing runs the gamut from illegal such as heroin to legal such as alcohol and tobacco. The line between harmful and legal and harmful and illegal is hard to set for two reasons. One is the libertarian argument that government should not tell you what to do at all. The other is that society is constantly changing its standards. Pornography is subject to constantly changing societal definitions. Not smoking made one as much of a social pariah in the fifties as smoking does today. The front line today shifts around such things as sugar or fatty foods. Even though the test of what things are harmful may be backed up by sound data from reputable studies, the subjective view of the society as to what interferes with their liberty drives the debate.

Societal groups fight constantly over the proper level of government protection.

 As soon as organizations were created to attain economic goals and societal goals, someone had to be in charge, make decisions, and direct actions. This led to the subordinate position. In a world where all men were of equal power, employment would be a matter of a willing labor buyer and a willing labor seller negotiating a market price for the services rendered. In such a case each receives what is desired at a reasonable price. The problem is that in such a system, no one gets everything. Accumulating control of everything seems to be what is desired by those who seek power and wealth.

Early on, in civilization, the desire to have everything resulted in the simple employer/employee relationship that exists in slavery. The progression is easy to see. Power begets power. As leadership progressed from elders to chiefs to kings, the size and complexity of the power grew. Wars over scarce resources, often in the form of territory, grew in scope. A form of feudalism developed, in which protection was offered in return for military service. Military service led to conquests, and conquests led to a ready source of cheap labor – slavery.

Slavery is the ultimate example of unchecked employer power. The only limit to that power was when the king ran up against an equal or stronger king, or when he overextended his ability to control already conquered areas. When conquest and slavery no longer provided sufficient labor, commercial forms of labor trade took over. Voluntary servitude grows out of desperate times. Loss of freedom looks better when compared to death by starvation.

In the fullness of time, slavery became a moral issue. It is no coincidence that the beginning of the end of slavery was simultaneous to the industrial revolution. Machinery was beginning to take up the slack. Production no longer required slaves. By the mid-19th century, the slavery issue was resolved in the U.S. and Britain. Nonetheless, it still exists in much of the world and in the sex trade even in America.

Industrialization and mass production led to factories and high labor productivity. Relatively high wages brought many from the farms to the factories. The struggle for greater power soon exerted itself. The hire–fire power of the employer ran rampant until a countervailing power of unions developed to provide some leverage to the seller of labor. Unions and collective bargaining resulted when the buyer of labor had an almost slave trader level of bargaining power in the market. The economic war was often punctuated by a hot war between the two sides. The struggle turned violent on both sides. The employer was usually supported by the police, the other by the proverbial union thugs.

It is often said that we live in the information age. It is a neat theory, but misses the fact that as of today, the information age had ended decades ago. Although exact dates are hard to pin down, the Stone

Age ended with the development of agriculture approximately 6,000 years ago. The Agriculture Age lasted for nearly 6,000 years until the beginnings of the industrial age started in earnest in the late 18th century. Machinery took over increasingly complex manual labor, a process that has yet to end. Then in the postwar era of the mid-20th century, just as machines had taken over manual labor, computers began to take over office and mental labor. This marked the beginning of the Information Age. What has been missed is that by approximately 1985, computers were able to perform all of the necessary tasks of the office. And nearly all useful information was readily available. Since that time, computer development has concentrated on graphics, speed, and non-essential activities.

So what era do we live in as of now? Call it what you will but it is an era dominated by advertising, public relations and entertainment. Is it the Advertising Age...the Entertainment age? Some might be tempted to call it the Communications Age, but with Twitter, Facebook, e-mail, smart phones, and other devices, people are communicating less than they ever did before in the lifetimes of our older citizens. Perhaps it should be called the Age of Shallowness.

One outfall of this has been a steady effort to eliminate the human being from the workforce. Beginning in the 1990s, this effort accelerated to a situation where business, in spite of all of the public relations to the contrary has been at war with humans, first employees and then customers. Eliminating head count was the mantra.

Ownership of machinery including computers, and software allowed for substantial redistribution of wealth from the lowly worker to the business owners. Service to customers was drastically reduced in order to increase profits. The self-service gas station was one simple logical step in this move to profits at the expense of customer service and employment.

But the looting of the employees and customers were not the only looting to take place in the economy. There still was the stockholder. Stockholders often include pension funds and small investors. Management bonuses were the mechanism by which they too could be looted.

Compensation to the non-productive side of the business (management) grew completely out of line with the productive side of business. Stockholder oversight got lost in sheer size.

Since the systematic elimination of people from the workforce is a continuing trend, it is not surprising to see a jobless recovery. It also allows profits to be achieved without work. Ownership is simply enough. Technology continues to replace human beings in the workforce.

Technological innovation is producing great things in medical care, energy and education. Even in those fields the replacement of people with technology remains a goal of profit seeking businesses. Ergo, technology continues in its trend of eliminating humans from the workplace. How then will society distribute the wealth if it is in no way related to work? We will reserve this question for a later part of the discussion.

Profits have always been crucial to the functioning of a society. Even pillaging other lands and kingdoms rewarded kings with profit from the labor of his armies. This continued through most of history up to and including the voyages of Francis Drake and his raids on Spanish shipping.

In addition to providing wages and jobs, business and commerce provide profits to the owners. Profits can then be used partially as compensation to the owners and to provide capital for the business growth. The growth allows the business to buy machinery, ships, planes, real estate, and inventory to leverage for even greater growth. In recent years, the movement to use capital for the purpose of eliminating humans from the workforce has accelerated to a very high degree.

The disconnect between contribution and reward continues to grow with this trend. The only thing necessary now to reap great reward is the ability to generate capital. Profits now become an even greater percentage of any revenues generated, and the effect snowballs like hotels on a monopoly board.

PART THREE
The Free Enterprise System

The free enterprise system is a system of economics that has been in effect since the beginnings of commerce. It is filled with problems, yet remains the only continuous viable system for business and commerce. As Winston Churchill once said about democracy, the free enterprise system is the worst system in the world, except when compared to all other systems. Indeed it could be argued that all other systems have been merely attempts to eliminate free enterprise, which is as natural as the rain.

Unfortunately, unchecked free enterprise becomes a monopoly game in which one person wins absolute economic power while everyone else goes broke, and it all hinges on a roll of the dice.

Of the two words in the system title, primacy has to go to the word free. Without the freedom to transact business, individual wants and needs tend to go unmet. Enterprise is also crucial, for without this part, wants and needs would continue to also go unmet. By what right should a government interfere with one individual's right to make a contract with another? In fact there are widely accepted reasons why government should interfere. Government has always stepped in to stop free transactions such as murder for hire, drug dealing, fraud, environmental destruction, and restraint of the rights of others to free trade. Some activities of government, including establishing a central bank, anti-trust, and national defense are actions taken that assist the operation of the free system.

Battle lines are still drawn between sides in today's debate about the limits of free enterprise, with many conservatives rising angrily at any limitation on the rights to make a profit regardless of how it may hurt others or the society in general. They imply that the only alternative to unchecked enterprise is communism. They do not believe in society caring for any of its weak or unfortunate citizens through its government.

If, on the other hand, they were to argue for a light hand of government regulation on the system, as had been done in the past, the argument that free enterprise does the best job of any system in providing for the needs of the citizenry would be unassailably correct. Today's conservatives do not seem to allow for careful and limited control or even cooperation and compromise with other elements within the society.

Deregulation in large part led to the crash and recession of 2008. This deregulation trend started during the Reagan years and continued through Clinton and beyond. We haven't learned our lesson yet, and who knows where it will lead. Inability to compromise on taxes greatly exacerbated the deficit problem and the debt problem. That lack of compromise continues and is growing worse. It is in stark contrast to the founding fathers, who built this great country and its constitution on compromise.

Since individual freedom stops where the freedom of another begins, it is not surprising that increased population tends to restrict freedom. It will be increasingly difficult for the rugged individualist portrayed by Ayn Rand to continue on without trampling the rights of others. The proximity of individuals creates a friction that must be controlled by some force, whether it be religion or government.

We live in a holistic society. It is so whether we like it or not, and we are all in this together. To say that a man or woman is only a creature of business or economic activity is too constrictive and inaccurate. They also are part of a family, a society, a religion, and any other group real or imagined. Our society is pluralistic. Man is also a spiritual being as opposed to just a physical one. All aspects of human nature must be considered when dealing with wealth or different economic systems.

Alternative Systems

As we have said, free enterprise is natural. Abuse of freedom is also natural. No system exists in its pure theoretical form. The choice between say communism and freedom is illusory. The issue is in varying shades on a spectrum between the two. It is not a hard and fast line, as many would have you believe today. Perhaps the price of freedom is economic disasters such as depressions and recessions. Another price is the maldistribution of wealth from producers to takers. The lack of widespread distribution of wealth is a characteristic of economic downturns. To have a well-functioning economy, it is necessary for wealth to be distributed to some extent. This creates markets for goods and services. Henry Ford knew that for sufficient Model T sales to generate profits, he had to build cars that could be afforded by the workers who made them.

Revolution has often been the end result of this poor distribution of wealth. When people have no other choice, they will often rise up in desperation. After the Russian revolution, the system of communism arose in an attempted solution to this problem. The theory was to completely control wealth and then to distribute it evenly, thus eliminating the social imbalances. It quickly degenerated into authoritarianism and totalitarianism. Why? It is because men seek power under any system. The concentration of economic power in a central government is the concentration of total power. It also eliminated economic motivation which resulted in a stifling of innovation and efficiency.

Communism had many proponents, and threatened to enslave the world from its inception to its practical end near the end of the 20th century. It failed, and as a practical system has been relegated to history. At its zenith, it controlled all of the Russian Empire and China, most of the world's population. Many call China a communist country, but that is simplistic. China still is not a free country, but has had to make many compromises to economic theory to support its population.

Socialism is a system in which the public in general, through their government, own the capital assets that produce the nation's wealth. The theory is that wealth will be distributed evenly through the society resulting in a general increase in the welfare of the people. There are two major problems with the theory. First, the concentration of power in the hands of the government without the countervailing power of business tends to lead to totalitarianism. Also, like communism, it takes away the incentive to produce.

Socialism, like communism, does not live up to the ideals that it propounds. As a system, it buckles under the weight of economic reality, and the pervasiveness of human turpitude. In its pure form, it leads to pure failure. Yet it continues to exist in impure form all around the world. When unchecked capitalism threatens the rich and powerful, governments will step in to save the business owners.

Sometimes, in the U.S. this has led to a limited form of "temporary" socialism with special subsidies, loans, and control. Of course business owners want to have the government money with no strings attached, but government bailouts usually don't work that way.

Capitalism is a system in which ownership of the means of production is held by people separate and apart from government. Some of the assets are owned collectively by retirement plans and other investment groups. Some are owned by individuals. That ownership and the power that goes with it tends to concentrate in the hands of fewer and fewer people until acted upon by some countervailing power, such as the another powerful capitalist, unions, the state, or a revolutionary body. Unbridled capitalism led to the stock market's sudden decline in 2008. Wall Street is not the greatest example of capitalism. Wall Street has found out how to siphon off large amounts of capital by trading between capitalists, without producing a single product.

Capitalism, like free enterprise, is a system that is amoral. Murder for hire and drug dealing are quite acceptable in a pure free enterprise system In such enterprises the capitalist would be the owner of the gun or the drug running airplane.

Any morality must come from outside of the free enterprise or capitalist system.

Although the system, without checks and balances lead to excesses, which lead to depressions, which lead to wars and revolutions, no other system comes close to providing for the citizens of a society the way free enterprise and capitalism does. Yet its success has come only because society, usually through government, has placed limits and boundaries on its operation.

Neither capitalism nor communism has existed for long in pure form. Survival of the society has come through a blending of systems. Black markets quickly develop in overly controlled economies. Likewise in capitalist countries, the public quickly cries for regulations to protect them from overreaching capitalist power brokers. The most successful capitalist system the world has ever known developed in America. The government provided a solid framework in which capitalism could operate. This included public safety, national defense, infrastructure, central banking and regulation. Recently, the government has stepped into environmental regulation to protect its citizens from the utter, complete, and irreversible destruction of the environment that could result from unchecked capitalism.

China arguably has been able to blend totalitarian government with a capitalist system. The vastness of Chinese culture simply overrides its totalitarian government with its innate mercantile sensibilities. With its size and economic gains, China has become a force to be reckoned with in the modern world. It has been a force for thousands of years, but for most of that time was isolated from the West.

It certainly seems that it is not possible to separate the political environment from the economic environment. Is it possible to have free commerce, where you do not have freedom of religion, political thought, or the press? It doesn't appear to. Much of the news from China indicates a gradual crumbling of its total control. We saw this in Russia. Technology only speeds up the process.

The United States has a different issue. In a democracy, the public has the right to think short term and vote for those measures which gain them short term benefits at the expense of the long term consequences. John Adams pointed out this problem early in our republic, in a letter from 1798. Growing deficits and the related increases in national debt are the results. Out of control national debt is not sustainable, and many a nation has fallen in the past when debt runs amok.

The second downfall of democracy, in addition to the ability of voters to destroy their grandchildren's future for their short term gain is the ease with which public opinion is manipulated by the unscrupulous. Modern communications and technology simply exacerbate this capability. For some reason large segments of the population are willing to surrender their right to think independently to an ideology, and mindlessly follow that ideology's propaganda.

The system of checks and balances built in to our constitution helps, but increasingly, it is seen as a danger to the self-interest of a large portion of our population. They rail against each of the branches of government depending on their politics. The President is good or bad depending on his party affiliation. Congress is corrupt except, of course, for your own elected representative who relentlessly fights that corruption. However, it is the "activist judges" on the Supreme Court that catch the most partisan ire. The Supreme Court is often only ruling on a single point of law, and how that law is interpreted. Each decision is then filtered through the ideology of the population before the wrath of the people is unleashed.

As flawed as it is, the free enterprise system should be preserved.

PART FOUR
The Society

Any economic or political system exists within the context of the society which surrounds it, and that society provides the basic framework for that system. The family usually provides the first organizational unit. If the family is the paramount social context, a political-economic system that attacks the family will be much more difficult to implement. Families grew into tribes and clans, but that organization was not enough. Throughout thousands of years of written human history, survival has depended on increasingly sophisticated organizations.

The desire for power and the desire for wealth are interchangeable. The earliest writing usually included the chronicles of great kings, but also included recordings of more mundane commercial activities. From the earliest records, we see economic and political activity existing side by side. From tribal elders to kings we see how power begat wealth and wealth begat power. Along with the power to judge between people, to make war, and to make decisions of life and death; kings accumulated great wealth, and many horses, servants and women.

Human labor was part of the spoils of victory. Frequently, kings would completely slaughter the conquered foe. Genocide was common. Terrorism and genocide were brought to a well-developed science by the ancient Assyrians. Offsetting this was the need for labor, so kings would bring back slaves from the conquered areas. In America, some tribes would take children of killed foe as their own. If the family remained a strong driver, such an action may have been motivated by compassion. These are examples of family and labor needs of the society driving the some of the ancient rules of war.

The cheap labor of slavery was one of the benefits of the wars, which cost so much in wealth and human life. A human life was a resource for the kings, and their societies. Slavery replaced and enhanced the labor supply, and the newly conquered lands enhanced the king's treasury, through natural resources and tributes.

A large part of the early social context of systems was the theocracy. Even though religion was central to social life in ancient societies, it was often little more than a tool by which men gained power. Religious leaders had power, and kings evoked religion to gain power. Indeed, many ancient conflicts were between peoples of different religious beliefs, and winning or losing was sometimes judged as a way to decide whose god or gods were more powerful. Theocracy still exists today. Sharia law is one example of theocracy. Wars, revolutions, dictatorships, suppression of women, strife and conflict accompany it wherever it goes. In the early days of the Massachusetts Colony, they adopted law that was a form of theocracy, in many ways resembling sharia law. Those executed as witches might think that this law was also suppression of women.

History continues to record political and economic systems existing side by side. In other words, wealth is often transferred by means outside the political power system. Businesses were able to exercise power and influence. As with today's campaign contributions, businesses had to be careful not to throw in too heavily with a king that might lose power through revolution and external conquest.

After the fall of the Roman Empire, the power of kings and emperors became diluted with the proliferation of states and smaller political units. China continued to have empire, but it was and remains diluted by the power of local leaders. During the Middle Ages feudalism exerted power locally. In exchange for protection, serfs willingly paid tribute in taxes and military service. Religious organizations often conducted business and commerce. The monks in European monasteries were the business barons of their time.

In a typically environmentally destructive quest for energy, they dammed English rivers, and polluted downstream areas with the effluence of their tanneries. England had one of the earliest attempts by government to induce environmental regulation as a result of this activity.

During the age of exploration, governments found themselves trying to grant franchises to protect investors as new lands opened up for exploitation. Businesses in turn tried to earn profits, often in trying circumstances on the frontiers of western civilization. Much conflict developed as those frontiers ran into other powerful civilizations in the east. Often, having travelled beyond the reach of their governments, they created their own sovereignty. This would ultimately morph into the American Revolution. Beyond the reach of government, armed conflict broke out between the Dutch East India Company and the Dutch West India Company. Business took on the role of government with unofficial declarations of war. Whether by business or government, the desire for power motivated men in a similar manner.

Capitalism has always existed, but the form of capital changed from land and slaves to machinery after the industrial revolution. This trend continued through the nineteenth and twentieth centuries. As the absolute power of kings and emperors diminished, the power of the owners of capital increased. As machinery replaced manual labor in everything from farming to manufacturing, the need for slaves also diminished. Although the value of interchangeable parts had been known for a long time, and frequently applied to firearms, it took the automobile to introduce true assembly line processing.

The repetitive nature of the assembly line quickly lent itself to mechanization. Land ownership took a back seat to factory ownership. The owners of factories were now the ones who accumulated wealth and power. They were not the only ones. Great fortunes were to be made in shipping, mining and railroads. In the earliest century of the United States, land remained a source of wealth. The Louisiana Purchase, the war with Spain, and the Indian wars led to an expansion of developable land by conquest and purchase.

Government provided the opportunities for the accumulation of wealth in the frontier. Policies that favored settlement and development included such things as the Homestead Act. Connecting that frontier by rail became a wellhead for the growth of personal wealth. Bankers and railroad barons, called robber barons by some, took advantage of the opportunities to accumulate great personal wealth. In return they provided the means for the west to grow and prosper. Let us not forget the contribution of imported Chinese labor. They received little personal reward beyond survival (and often not even that) with their virtual slave labor contribution.

However, technology never stood still. Those in the right place and time were able to take advantage of the new automobile technology. Now great fortunes could be accumulated in oil, auto manufacturing, and road building. Being able to capitalize quickly on developing technology continues today. Knowing when to exit the market is as important as knowing when to jump in. Witness the dot-com bubble, which distorted stock markets then burst at the end of the 20th century.

Often monopolies and government franchises gave opportunities for power accumulation. Once monopoly was established, a chance to receive reward far in excess of contribution was also established. Great fortunes could now be had. The struggle between the desire for monopoly and the public effort through government to control monopolistic and cartel behavior has not ended since it came to the forefront during the administration of Teddy Roosevelt.

Investment banking, once it was deregulated provided a great opportunity for people to become wealthy without contributing. In fact the contribution of Wall Street was such a substantial negative that it nearly destroyed the American economy and threatened the economy of the entire world. In spite of the vast and sweeping negative contribution of the Wall Street investment bankers, they were handsomely rewarded with great personal wealth for their turpitude.

The desire for power is universal among men and women. All of human history shows the effects of this universal desire. Remember, wealth is power and power is wealth. From the tribal leader, to kings to emperors to presidents to CEOs, this drive to achieve power over other members of the human race is pervasive and palpable. The perception of a lack of power leads to revolutions and civil rights movements. Women's liberation was just one more manifestation of the desire to increase power over the lives of others. Women wanted power and perceived that men had it. Civil rights movements are often not about justice and equality, but simply a non-altruistic power struggle by a different name.

It seems to be a common belief that only people of European descent desire power over their fellow man, but history shows that no race or culture is immune to this universal drive. From Nero to Genghis Kahn to Shaka Zulu, only the locations change.

It is also important to note that not every human on the planet seeks power. Although history is written in blood by those who seek power, the growth of human civilization has come from the billions of nameless men and women who worked the farms, factories, transportation facilities, or banks. Some may desire power but are unwilling to pay the moral price necessary to achieve it to any degree. With notable exceptions, whether in politics or business the scrupulous will usually lose out to the ruthless. Most people want to do the right thing. They accept that others are struggling for wealth and power. They go to bed each night to sleep peacefully while the battle for power rages outside. This is a good thing. It is such people who make the world work.

PART FIVE
Mergers, Acquisitions, and Privatization

The theory of mergers and acquisitions is that, through economies of scale brought about by those mergers and acquisitions, the customers and employees will be better served. The reality of such transactions is that everybody loses but the surviving top managements. If nearly everyone loses, why merge? The activity is driven by the same desire for power that kings and emperors had long ago. The desire for power and wealth is never sated, and regardless of how big the company is, top management wants more. This insatiable desire has been with us for thousands of years of human history.

Whether it is banking, railroads, manufacturing, or retail, the story is the same. As business grows, it becomes more inefficient in its organization. Bureaucracy is a function of size. After a tipping point somewhere around 300-500 employees, the organization's energies are swallowed up by efforts at internal communication and office politics. Employees become more dedicated to their relative positions in the organization than to organizational goals. Bureaucracy is an attempt to control internal communication and activity, but it also acts as a drag on the energy and creativity of the people. The federal government is not bureaucratic because it is government but because it is big. It is always put forth as the epitome of inefficiency.

The first losers in mergers and acquisitions are the employees.

Mergers and acquisitions allow business the opportunity to downsize to eliminate duplication. Although redundant departments can be eliminated, much of the work is not duplicated. This allows the business to demand more work out of its remaining employees and usually with less pay. The threat of downsizing is used to demand total loyalty above family, church, or any outside life. It is little more than the slave driver's whip to employees.

The second loser in these transactions is the customer.

Two other things occur with mergers and acquisitions. The supply of competitors is reduced, and the customer is further isolated by the size of the organization. The company is now free to pour more money into public relations to tell people how good they are while eliminating budget items that might increase customer service. It is also free to do what bigness does best in business, raise more capital.

Although customer service is hard to truly measure, anecdotally few people feel that they really receive better service with the new and bigger entity. There is little or no evidence that mergers and acquisitions lead to better service.

Indiana National Bank was a major commercial bank in Indianapolis. It was purchased by the National Bank of Detroit in 1992. INB was well advanced in its IT systems, and especially in customer service. NBD was far behind. Since they were the surviving bank, all systems had to be converted to their system. Surviving and taking firms typically are unwilling to learn from the taken firm. It is reminiscent of the conquest of one people by another in ancient times.

Sometimes even the stockholder loses.

This is more problematic since top management is often a major stockholder in one of the organizations, and may hold stock options. If the business is dismantled, and/or spun off, great care must be taken to see that the people making the transaction are protected. Remember, in these transactions, management is working for their own interest, not the interest of the companies involved. There must be a quick take away of money that cannot be returned in the event of collapse of the new entity. Bonuses are often the best way to accomplish this.

Also, we should not forget the role of investment bankers and lawyers. They make their money by a process that they call "churning deals." Whether the deals are good or bad is of little interest, since they get their money just by making the deal happen. Big deals result in big takeaways, with no responsibility or accountability for what happens in the future. Like land developers, they can take their money and run.

Society as a whole also loses. When the customer loses his service and pays more for it, when unemployment increases, when taxes are lost, and when wealth redistributes from the productive to the unproductive, the society has lost. An uneven distribution of wealth is something that is commonly found in recessions and depressions. It is the redistribution of wealth to fewer and fewer at the top that is the ultimate goal of mergers and acquisitions.

The big winners are the lawyers, investment bankers, and top management

Privatization

Privatization is a form of corporate takeover in which the takeover target is an organization that serves the public interest. In the United States there is a well-established distrust of government. From the American Revolution to Will Rogers, it is deeply engrained in the American psyche. This distrust is a rich mother lode to be mined by self-serving politicians.

Privatization is also a form of patronage on a grander scale. Under the patronage system, politicians give public jobs to those who support them by their contributions or their efforts. The civil service was an attempt to populate government workers with qualified people instead of unqualified political hacks. Privatization allows for entire public service functions to be given to those in favor. Only legally required bid and proposal requirements stand in the way.

The theory of privatization is that businesses are efficient and government is inefficient. The theory also says that because there is no competition in provision of government services, there is no incentive for efficiency. Further, people do not work efficiently without the motivation that comes by threat of losing your job to the competition. The biggest problem with the theory is that none of these things are true. Public employees work as hard and as intelligently as private employees.

If the politicians have been so unsuccessful at managing their responsibilities, that they have to hire a private company to manage their constituents' needs, it means that they have failed in their duty to the public. It is only an example of their own incompetence. If the core competence of a politician is to get elected, it is not surprising that he or she would be incompetent at management.

Logic alone says that adding profits into the cost of performing public services only increases the cost of those services. They could be run more efficiently by the application of good management without siphoning off a profit margin. Reality intrudes whenever privatization is attempted. For one thing, public services do not tend to be inherently profitable. Police and fire protection, services that care for the helpless, infrastructure open to all without excessive tolls, national defense, education and regulation are not profit generating enterprises. However, those are all necessary for the society to survive in modern times. An enterprise fund run in the public interest can generate a profit, but this profit should remain in public hands. It should not be sold for a short-term capital infusion and deprive the citizens of the profits that should rightly be theirs in the future.

One problem with privatization is that businesses come and go, merge and spin off, and file bankruptcy. Even if a city or state files bankruptcy, it still exists and has to function in some manner. Public officials can be held accountable. A business just disappears and there is no accountability for mismanagement.

Anotherproblem is the process of cream skimming. In the case of privatized education and prisons, private companies often take only the very best students or prisoners. They can then claim good results since they are not burdened with the need to provide for the needs of all the citizenry. Businesses must make a profit. Efforts to squeeze profits (and bonuses) from unprofitable public services result in increased costs and decreased services to the public.

It is hard to find an example in the U.S. of privatization of public function being successful, where success is defined as better service, lower cost, or any combination of the two.

Indianapolis, Indiana privatized its water treatment. Shortly after that, there were two major fish kills where there had never been any before. They privatized golf courses. Soon the facilities deteriorated. They privatized the airport. Inefficiency ran rampant. Much of the inefficiency was masked by the fact that pre-privatization activity was paying dividends when the private operator started. Since airlines were the biggest losers in the airport deal, the general public was unaware of the inefficiency.

Prisons in Texas and Louisiana have been privatized. In Louisiana this led to higher incarceration rates, since law enforcement had now become entrepreneurs. The more people were kept in prison, the more profits were generated.

The information that the public receives about privatization is carefully controlled in an informal ideological conspiracy. The public is blissfully unaware of how much of their money is being lost to privatization schemes. Politicians win because they claim non-existent efficiencies. Business owners win because they make profits and bonuses from the process. As with mergers and acquisitions, the lawyers also win. The losers are the customers in the case of enterprise funds such as toll roads, and taxpayers for other schemes such as parking meters. A proposal to privatize social security is a perennial favorite. Wall Street salivates at the possible opportunity to loot social security revenues.

Books and articles that tout privatization are always before the public eye. One such book, Reinventing Government, was instrumental in kicking off a privatization craze. It talks of all of the supposed savings through privatization. Much of the claimed savings of privatization is based on phrases like "projects that", "thinks that", "expects to", "believes it will", and "hopes to" There is little or no true and unbiased evidence of savings from privatization.

Often the definition of privatization has been tweaked to include privatization of businesses in Russia, or decentralization of airports in Canada. Then these cases were used to show success in privatization. In the case of Russia, it privatizing what was really a private function to begin with. In the case of Canadian airports, it was merely decentralization, not a privatization. The many failures of privatization are carefully swept under the rug. What politician is going to say "oops, we really screwed up?" In all there has been a massive campaign to sell the idea to unsuspecting taxpayers, and it has been an easy sell.

PART SIX
A World Without Work

Since the beginning of man, work has defined our existence and been the means of accumulation of wealth and power. Whether chipping out a clovis arrowhead or killing game, it was work that created and claimed wealth. Apples lying on the ground in the wild were not anyone's wealth. From Adam Smith forward, it was accepted that the work of picking up those apples created a person's claim to them.

If you were fortunate enough to survive conquest, the institution of slavery provided subsistence. In some cases slavery even provided upward mobility. What slavery did do was allow some to thrive without production and rely on slaves to provide for their needs and wants. The system allowed for the establishment of an upper class supported by a lower class.

The first transformation of the economic world came with agriculture. The change from hunting and gathering to farming ushered in the Agrarian Age. This Age was to last six to ten thousand years. Future major shifts would come much more quickly. During the Agrarian Age, wealth accrued to the owners of the land. Whether acquired through conquest or purchase, it was the ultimate source of wealth. The ability to produce enough food to support an idle upper class was a major societal driver. From Pharaoh to the plantation owners in the 18th and 19th centuries, it was the basic building block of wealth and a class society.

The end of the Agrarian Age came with the industrial revolution. The transformation of commerce and society came when the need for manual labor began to diminish. From farms to factories, machinery took over the basic tasks of planting, harvesting, manufacturing, and transportation.

The Industrial Age lasted from the late 18th century until its zenith in the 1940s. It was here that industry was applied with full force to win the Second World War and then produce consumer goods in abundance in the 1950s. The process of converting labor to machinery never stopped during the entire Industrial Age. The Industrial Age lasted only about 150 years.

Although machinery was doing the work of manual labor, there was still much office work to be accomplished. It was in the 1950s and 1960s that the computer began to eliminate office work. The typing pool, stenographers, secretaries, and bookkeepers were targeted for mechanization. This was the beginning of what was to become known as the Information Age. At first computers were good for extremely complex scientific calculations and for high volume activity such as existed in the banking and insurance industries. They took up complete rooms that required special air conditioning to function.

Soon, they became "mini-computers" that were the size of a desk. Quickly they morphed into desktops, laptops, and hand held smart phones. The internet allowed quick access to information, both true and false.

As previously discussed, many believe that we are still in the Information Age, but I submit that the Information Age ended in1985. Why 1985? By that time computers had reached the point in which all information that was useful was available. All calculations that needed to be done, excepting some scientific work, could easily be done. Future development was more for graphics, entertainment and show than for real work. If I am correct, the Information Age lasted only about 30 years.

So what Age are we now in? I am torn between calling it the Sales Age or the Entertainment Age, or perhaps the Age of Shallowness. That encompasses both of the previous names mentioned. We are in a ceaseless bombardment of sales messages, easily jammed in front of our eyes by technology. Public relations and propaganda are also advertising in that they are aimed at manipulating your thoughts to achieve the purposes of the person or entity producing the image. Businesses are willing to spend millions to tell people how good their customer service is while at the same time are unwilling to put pennies into their budget to actually provide good customer service.

Our economy hinges entirely on our ability to sell people things that they don't need.

There is still work to be provided in the service industry. Outsourcing has become a means of dumping any corporate responsibility for taking care of its employees. The firms providing the outsourced labor can now hire desperate workers at little pay and no benefits, it reduces cost to the outsourcing firm. It is a return to the voluntary servitude system. Outsourcing is also a way of reducing accountability for serving the customer.

Gambling is another means of transferring wealth from the many to the few. It used to be that in the U.S. one had to go to Nevada or Atlantic Beach to gamble. Now it is pervasive, and the odds are always with the house. Lotteries are in many states and they reinforce the idea that people will not achieve wealth by work. This may be an accurate message, but taxing by lottery may not be the answer. Indeed wealth is no longer achieved by work but by wheeling and dealing in some commodity (including money) without making a contribution to society.

There is still work in service industries, medicine, and education. Yet inroads are being made in those areas as quickly as possible with such things as teleconferenced classrooms, self-diagnosis hospital admissions, and classroom computers. We humans are clever and it seems that there is little or nothing that cannot be turned over to a computer or a robot. Indeed the technology exists to eliminate the need for driving, and for truck drivers.

It is easily possible to conceive of a world without productive work to do, since it is all done by machine. How would such a world look? How would wealth be distributed?

Assuming that enough meaningful work would be done by automation to virtually eliminate the need for work, and that the world would have adequate provisions, there are several possible scenarios:

First Scenario

Mankind would distribute all of its resources so that no one would want. All would be equal in provisions under thi utopian society. The reason it is not communism is that, with plentiful supplies, there would be no need for government enforcement. The wealthy class that owns the means of production, would provide for the rest of society by their charity. This scenario is unlikely because human history tells us that the desire to be wealthier than your neighbor would lead to an eventual imbalance and related turmoil. Further, such a world would be devoid of ambition and motivation, a dull and lifeless world indeed. Amusing ourselves with entertainment would be all that is left for us to do. Aldous Huxley speculated on how such a world would look in his book *Brave New World*.

Second Scenario

Since there would presumably be owners of the production technologies, they alone would have all of the wealth and keep it to themselves. The rest would starve. Some of the other citizens would be kept around for the amusement of the wealthy class. Human nature alone would lead one to believe that this would be a more likely scenario than expecting the wealthy to distribute their wealth. How can you live in greater luxury, if everyone around you has the same luxuries?

Third Scenario

The desire to have more than your fellow man would win out to the point that wars and revolutions would prevail. The drive to take from others even though there is plenty for all, would lead to unlimited conflicts. Power begets power and we would be back where we started with tribal disputes and kings or emperors vying for control. History would have come full circle.

Fourth Scenario

The public distributes wealth through its government. This is communism implemented in the context of plenty. Loss of freedom would result. However, a burgeoning police and courts system would at least provide some employment.

In *Animal Farm*, George Orwell points out the human propensity for prospective leaders to claim they can provide a better future than those presently in charge. Once they get in power, they become the very thing they had previously railed against. Orwell goes on to write of a dark and dreary communist society *(1984)* in which the government takes and relentlessly holds power. Aldous Huxley sees a drugged out loveless society with basic needs being met *(Brave New World)*. Of the two visions, *Brave New World* would seem to be closest to a world without work, and it is an unsatisfying world at best.

None of these possibilities so far is particularly pleasant. But wait, there's more. Regardless of the ability to provide for the requirements of life without work, the planet is limited to the resources that exist on the planet. The potential population, absent a mitigating factor, is infinite. As man squeezes an infinite population onto a finite planet, resources will eventually run out. That is more than just oil and metals. It is productive land, potable water, and even breathable air. Certainly, some Malthusian event would take over long before that happened. War, famine and pestilence would thin the herds of humans until a balance of nature is restored.

With the legalization of abortion in the United States, we have already shown a willingness to terminate another human life because that human's existence would be an inconvenience to us. This issue has never been about "women's reproductive rights". If you argue that a fetus is not human, what makes you so sure? Euthanasia is then but a small philosophical step from abortion. China's one child policy is an affront to freedom, human rights and human dignity. It is innate in man to know when something is wrong, as we will discuss in the next section. Still, a long term solution eludes us. Respect for human life would seek a less violent solution, but one thing is known: something will give somewhere.

Thus far mankind has had a frontier to fill. The propensity for man to soil his campground by destroying his environment is well established. A planet filled to capacity will be very difficult to manage, even without meaningful work to do.

What can save us?

PART SEVEN
Morality and Religion

Man is a spiritual creature. Where is the person you knew when the body lays in the coffin? What is missing is the spirit. That spirit exists in as many forms as there are people, and it shows through the expressions and actions of the body. The idea of holistic medicine acknowledges this, and as a result has had many medical successes. Societies also have a kind of spirit that results from the collective actions of the spirits that make up the societal body.

From the earliest times religion has played a major part in society. Does morality come from religion, or is it something that is hardwired into mankind? Is morality merely enlightened self-interest? How does religion enter into the perception of wealth and power? Does religion control the means of attaining wealth and power? Just as religion influences humanity, human ambition influences religion.

For the most part, men and women want to do the right thing as they understand it. Most people want to work, care for their family, and live life without a driving need to control others. The ambition to have power and financial superiority over others exists in enough people that it shapes and molds societies and nations.

It also corrupts religion. This corruption has manifested itself in religious wars, conquests, the crusades, and the inquisition. Corrupted religion results in vast religious hierarchies, state religions, and great power in the church. For many centuries theocracies made many political decisions. Some of the manifestations of this are sharia law or religious splits that happen because some powerful king wanted something. This can be seen from the emperor Constantine, to the Holy Roman Empire, to Henry the Eighth.

On the other hand, religion can act as a check and balance against unbridled human passions and desires. It can keep people in line. Considering the nature of the spirit, religion takes into account the possibility that there could be a future beyond the grave. This is not merely the opiate that controls the masses; it is hope, and a reason to not unleash your desires on the rest of the world. Cynical power mongers have often used religion to further their quest for power and wealth.

Most religions encourage benevolence toward those who have been less fortunate. Love places limits on power. Love places limits on the use of wealth. Some view monasticism or asceticism as a way to avoid the corrupting influence of wealth. Some of the founding fathers of the U.S. realized the importance of religion in a democracy. Jefferson and Adams argued about the need for government to control the evil nature of man. I imagine that both men would be surprised at the secularization of today's society. Government is needed now more than ever as the stabilizing influence of religion wanes.

Much is said about wealth in the Christian Bible, mostly in relation to its illusory and transitory nature in view of eternity. In the Jewish scriptures (the Christian Old Testament) Solomon was quite knowledgeable about wealth and power. He had accumulated horses, wealth and women far beyond the imagining of most of the world's most powerful and wealthy kings at the time. He calls it unsatisfying and just vanity.

Christ has much to say about wealth. Without condemning wealth and power per se, He places it in the perspective of eternity. It exists for a moment and passes with life. It can become an overpowering addiction that leads to an insatiable desire. It can be placed before the desire for the afterlife. He indicates that it is very difficult for a rich man to keep that perspective. C. S. Lewis points out that wealth knits man to the present world. Indeed it makes it difficult to concentrate on the next life.

The moneylenders in the temple, the Wall Street bankers of that time and place, simply profited from trade without contributing. Christ drove them from the temple. He called them thieves. This is strong language for these businessmen who traded on the noble desires of the customers to provide sacrifices to their God.

Christ echoes Solomon's point that all of this is temporal. It is more important not to violate the laws of God, since the prescribed penalty for that is death. Yet the Christian Bible is also clear that everyone violates those laws. The standard is exceptionally high.

In the end, Christ lays down his own life in order to pay the penalty for man's violation of God's laws. What better statement of the temporal nature of physical existence. In all of history or literature there has never been a better, albeit unattainable, example to live by.

All religions practice a form of charity. This keeps man in contact with his fellow beings that are less fortunate. All religions have some form of morality. The morality of religion is a force that has kept so much of mankind from breaking down into a free-for-all of unbridled personal ambition.

It is true that religion has not prevented, and has even augmented much of man's inhumanity toward man. The wars and genocides of ancient times did not end in ancient times because the desire for power did not end with ancient times.

Morality keeps the desire for wealth at the expense of others in check. By the same token, the desire for wealth at the expense of others often drives morality into the background.

The increased secularization of the western world has left a void in moral constraints. It is here that enlightened self-interest has manifested itself by the people through government. In the United States, government has stepped in with regulations ranging from efforts to prevent environmental destruction to efforts to prevent fraud. After the Great Depression, regulations to prevent the excesses that led to it were put in place. As those were dismantled, the steady march to another major recession began, and 2008 followed.

Government has not yet imposed a moral code as effective as that imposed by some religions.

PART EIGHT
A Solution

If the means of production are in the hands of a few, work is no longer required, and religion fades, what could happen? History tells us that it is unlikely that the wealthy and powerful will distribute to all based on their largesse. Other alternatives are starvation, communism or revolution. With all of the dreary possibilities for the future, shouldn't there be a solution? Considering that man has dealt with economic systems for thousands of years without coming up with the perfect solution, it is certainly doubtful that I can. However, it might be a good idea to look at a few possibilities, and perhaps come up with an approach. We can certainly eliminate some possibilities in order to leave them on the scrapheap of history and not waste any more time with them.

First, free societies have a long track record of better serving their citizens than societies that are not free. There are many reasons for this. Freedom allows for the full realization of talents. Freedom allows for a modicum of contentment, which in turn allows for creativity and enterprise. Having established that, how can a framework of morality be put in place if man's inherent need for morality has failed internally?

Further, the free enterprise system requires a societal framework to function. Free enterprise functions well when government provides the infrastructure, defense, police and fire protection, education, a banking system and moral constraints in the form of regulation.

Are there limits to freedom? Fortunately, the founding fathers realized that there are limits. At the same time as they romanticize the founding fathers, many of today's conservatives have abandoned the founding fathers and the constitution in a desperate effort to eliminate government implementation of moral constraints on society. Yet individual freedom ends where it abuts the freedom of others. Each believes that his freedom supersedes the freedom of those around him. This is why we have courts to judge between people. Again courts are provided by governments which are so hated by today's conservatives.

Consider ways in which government has overregulated commerce. Murder for hire is a business which, if done with impunity, provides the business owner with a profit while providing the customer with the product he desires. Government steps in and prohibits this commercial trade. Drug dealing is another profitable trade which satisfies the customers' desires. This also is prohibited by the intrusive government. Fraud is a profitable enterprise, but really does not serve the customer. Pyramid schemes are a particular brand of fraud which seems as if it will expand forever. Eventually these schemes collapse, and many lose while a few profit greatly.

Since we have established a level of control that government should legitimately exercise over commerce, the next step would be to define the limits of that control. Since a basic principal is that government should not impose limitations on free transactions between willing parties unless absolutely necessary, the lines become murky. Free enterprise will self-destruct without a government framework of operation. Unfair and immoral practices leading to monopoly and unrestricted power, would effectively end opportunity for free enterprise. Government tries to protect fair trade and freedom. This is government interference to protect the system. It is complicated and messy, but necessary.

There is not a consistent definition of morality in America. Government enforces as best it can the inconsistent and constantly changing view of morality held by its citizens. The citizens in turn are in violent disagreement on morality. Another problem with the democratic system and the free enterprise system is that the citizenry views only the shortest term good with complete disregard for the long term consequences. Government is of little help in solving this problem since it becomes part of the problem. Absent a leap of education, sophistication and maturity on the part of the populace this problem will not be solved.

Inflicting human suffering for personal gain seems to be widely accepted as a no-no. Yet when the economic reward becomes great enough, businesses will poison the air and water for profit, bankers will take great risks with depositors' money, and unsafe products will be rushed to market. The population in general may suffer great financial or physical loss to enhance the coffers of the wealthy and powerful.

After observing the workings of business from all sides, I perceive at least four discernible laws that apply to the activities of large organizations. They are especially applicable to business activity.

Boone's Law #1
There is nothing so simple that it cannot be made complicated.

Boone's Law #2
The more a business talks about concern for the customer, the less real concern it has for the customer.

Boone's Law #3
Where truth is not valued, lies will prevail.

Boone's Law #4

The purpose of business is the transference of wealth from the customer, the employee, and sometimes the stockholder to top management.

Given all of the negative drivers that exist in human nature, is there a solution. I suggest that the solution to the problem of today's business and commerce lies only within the society itself. The society will either have to regulate commerce itself or have government regulate commerce for it. What if a completely new approach to business was accepted from the CEO to the lowliest employee? What if ethics and social responsibility were truly conveyed in business school? Based on so many businessmen and managers that I have met; business schools are doing a very poor job of conveying any concept of ethics.

The results of such a self-controlled system might be a world of businesses, in which the businesses actually were the entities that are portrayed in their public relations announcements and their advertising. What if they really did care about the customer? What if they did not browbeat their long suffering employees about customer service, and instead gave them budgets that would allow them to serve the customer? What if customer service was more important than management salaries and bonuses?

What if they adopted from Hippocrates a philosophy of "do no harm"?

I hasten to add that I believe there are businesses that do this. I have dealt with such businesses, and I also believe that they are successful at generating profits. Reasonable profit is within reach of an ethical and customer focused business. The excessive profits and bonuses of other businesses can bring a whole economy down, as we have seen frequently on Wall Street.

A better business model is within reach if the society can bring it about through dialogue. The conservatives would have to talk to the liberals, something that is not happening today. This could solve the problems inherent in business and commerce. Sure, many of those with the greatest wealth would not be able to accumulate as much, but there would still be adequate motivation and society as a whole would prosper.

As for the population/environment problem, people may also self-regulate. Absent that, nature will solve the problem for us. Government cannot solve this problem. China tried this with its one-child policy, and it was a great affront to human dignity and to freedom. It has failed.

An educated populace can solve problems if the politicians and the press allow it to happen.

PART NINE
A Truly Wealthy Person

What is a truly wealthy person? Do we understand the true nature of wealth? Can our actions enhance or improve the lives of other individual members of society and make them more self-fulfilled? Remember improvement of our existence does not mean the elimination of all of the things that try and test us during our lives. Eliminating work will not make our lives better. Eliminating adversity and challenge will not make our lives better. Perspective and contentment make life better.

The apostle Paul said he had learned to be content in plenty and in want. Whether he was well provided for at the time or in prison, he was not cowed by his situation.

We need only to remember a few things to improve our existence and the society in which we live:

Wealth is a measure of what a person takes from society and keeps for himself not a measure of contribution.

As a society we should learn to value contribution. Instead of admiring people like Donald Trump for what he has accumulated, we should admire people like Henry Kaiser for what he has contributed. Beyond the contribution of the wealthy and powerful, we should consider the contribution of the farmer, the worker, and the public servant even though their compensation is less. We should eschew all negative contributions whether from Wall Street or the lowest street crime drug dealer. Too often we have envy and admiration for the successful taker.

Our goal should be to become givers not takers. Only if the positive contribution of the contributors exceeds the negative contribution of the takers will society function, and if it exceeds by a large amount the society will thrive. America thrives because of the positive contribution of its citizens.

The world is filled with good people. Consider the sacrifices of so many in our military, who have contributed their very lives to protect the country and others around the world who strive for a better world.

No one should be ashamed of not having wealth. We should be ashamed of not contributing. Not striving solely for wealth is not a call for sloth. Instead, the striving should be for contribution to the common good of the organization and society. Hopefully in the end efforts for the positive will outweigh the negative results. The good is worth fighting for.

The free enterprise system must be preserved.

No other system works. Yet without constraints, free enterprise carries the seeds of its own destruction. It will self-destruct unless contained. Today government provides the basic framework that allows the system to work. Overregulation impedes the effective working of the system, but no regulation at all brings its complete downfall.

It is a worthy effort to eliminate regulation that is burdensome, ineffective, and counterproductive. The public debate should be about where the lines should be drawn. This is a worthy discussion. The polarization of the society by politicians and the press has shut down discussion and debate on the subject. The conservatives of today have virtually ended rational discussion of the issues, and the flames of passion without rational thought are fanned by conservative talk show hosts.

To preserve freedom in our country, especially freedom of commerce, the debate must be joined. It is not necessary to live in a country or world where the air, land and seas are poisoned, where hard work is without reward, where the unfortunate are left to die. An effort to relate contribution to reward would pay great dividends to a future society.

Remember that government cannot change society. It cannot create morality but only can enforce morality. Morality and ethics must come from society itself. This is especially critical in a democracy.

One further note concerning the system: We should teach ourselves and our children to look beyond the next quarter's earnings, beyond the next election, and even beyond our own lives. Somewhere along the linewe have lost all thought of the future and sacrificed it for short term gain. This would have to change.

A world without work is coming, if not already here.

High unemployment is a condition of our times. There are fewer and fewer jobs for workers, and those jobs can be eliminated by the judicious deployment of technology. As discussed, a new way of distributing wealth will have to be devised since it will not accrue based on work. Actually work has not been the road to wealth for a long time. Only wheeling and dealing and trading have been the way to vast wealth. This inevitably leads to great concentrations of wealth and ultimately to the class society of kings and serfs – right back where we started.

Fairness should be the standard. Needs and altruism must also be taken into consideration. With a growing population chasing increasingly scarce resources such as air and water, survival may ultimately depend on the ability to wage war effectively.

Should that be the goal? If you were on a lifeboat with only enough food and water for a few, would you kill your fellow travelers by lottery or some other criteria; or would you all agree to live and die together without making the life and death judgment?

It is our choice.

We will decide how we will handle the future even when we cannot control it. Society makes business and government. Society must come together if the problems are to be solved or mitigated. Although both good and evil exist in the hearts of men, individuals must work on their own heart. The success or failure of America, society, and the world will come from the hearts of men and women.

Each person can achieve at the very least an element of internal contentment. Admiration of and desire for personal wealth damages the individual and society.

If perchance wealth should come your way, do not turn it down. It should not be a source of shame. Neither should it be a source of pride. Serving others brings a degree of peace and contentment. The chronicle of the American dream is not the Wall Street Journal. The American dream is larger, broader and greater than money and wealth. It is written in the efforts of all who go to work each day, solve problems and serve. America was built by generations of farmers, businessmen, doctors, laborers, slaves, builders, ministers, engineers, lawyers, warriors, nurses, waitresses, homemakers, teachers, artists, entertainers, coolies, policemen, firefighters, janitors, social workers, and many others that contributed more than they took. They are the ones to be admired.

About the Author

Alan Boone lives in Indianapolis, Indiana and is a graduate of Wabash College, where he majored in Economics. He worked in the airport industry in Indiana and North Carolina. He is an Accredited Airport Executive (A.A.E.) and retired from forty years in the airport industry in 2011. During most of that time, he served as CFO for the Indianapolis Airport Authority, and was able to observe first-hand the workings of business and government. He and his wife Sandy have three children, and eight grandchildren.